Great Kitchen De

A Visual Feast of Ideas and Resources

Tina Skinner

Schiffer Publishing Ltd

4880 Lower Valley Road, Atglen, PA 19310 USA

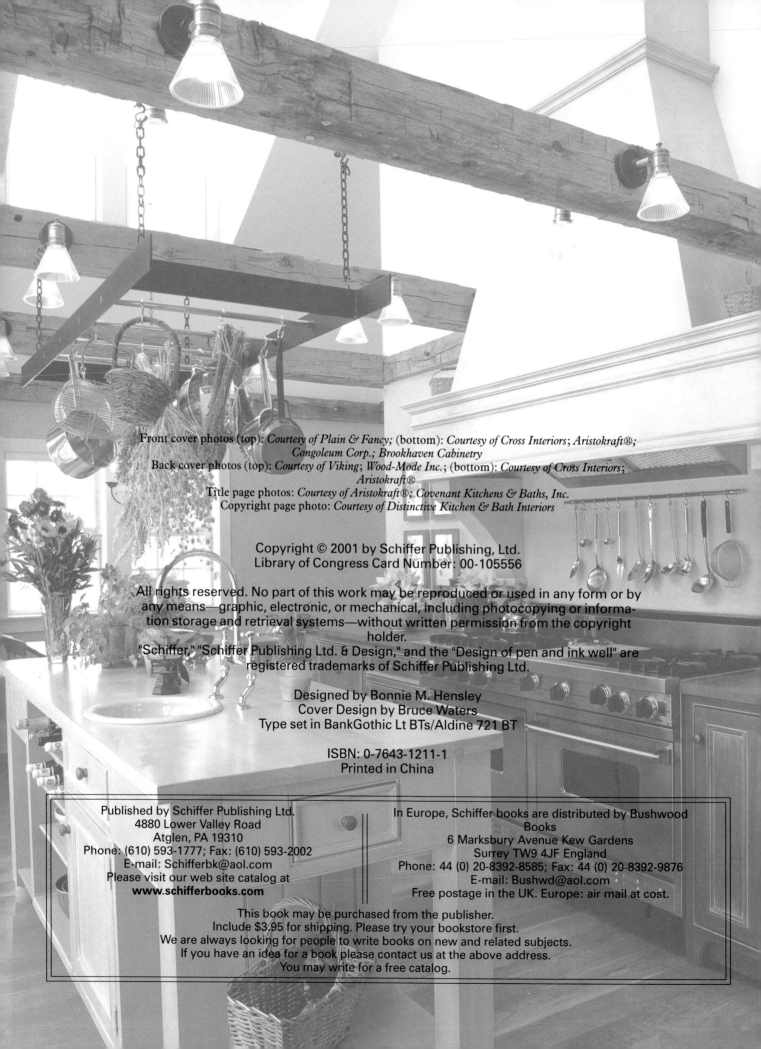

Front cover photos (top): *Courtesy of Plain & Fancy;* (bottom): *Courtesy of Cross Interiors; Aristokraft®; Congoleum Corp.; Brookhaven Cabinetry*
Back cover photos (top): *Courtesy of Viking; Wood-Mode Inc.;* (bottom): *Courtesy of Cross Interiors; Aristokraft®*
Title page photos: *Courtesy of Aristokraft®; Covenant Kitchens & Baths, Inc.*
Copyright page photo: *Courtesy of Distinctive Kitchen & Bath Interiors*

Designed by Bonnie M. Hensley
Cover Design by Bruce Waters
Type set in BankGothic Lt BTs/Aldine 721 BT

ISBN: 0-7643-1211-1
Printed in China

Published by Schiffer Publishing Ltd.
4880 Lower Valley Road
Atglen, PA 19310
Phone: (610) 593-1777; Fax: (610) 593-2002
E-mail: Schifferbk@aol.com
Please visit our web site catalog at
www.schifferbooks.com

In Europe, Schiffer books are distributed by Bushwood Books
6 Marksbury Avenue Kew Gardens
Surrey TW9 4JF England
Phone: 44 (0) 20-8392-8585; Fax: 44 (0) 20-8392-9876
E-mail: Bushwd@aol.com
Free postage in the UK. Europe: air mail at cost.

This book may be purchased from the publisher.
Include $3.95 for shipping. Please try your bookstore first.
We are always looking for people to write books on new and related subjects.
If you have an idea for a book please contact us at the above address.
You may write for a free catalog.

Courtesy of Restore 'N More/Barbara Herr

CONTENTS

Acknowledgments

One need only look at the Resource Guide at the back of this book to see who contributed. Special thanks also go to professional photographer Jim Fiora of Wallingford, Connecticut, who contributed photos. His work can also be seen online at www.jimfiora.com. Special thanks as well to photographer David Schilling of Atlanta, Georgia, who also contributed photos. Thanks also to Helen Ciaramitaro of The Hardwood Council, who managed to dig up even more images for me and provide me with additional sources after I sacked her archives for my first book on kitchen design; to the independent designers who went the extra mile, and expense, to help me with this project; to the Kitchen Cabinet Manufacturers Association and the Tile Council of America for invaluable leads; and to my husband, Craig Sibol, who pitched in as my dissatisfaction with our own kitchen grew. He agreed to move a very heavy old butcher block, our antique china cabinets, and an entire dining set, and when I ripped apart a wall against his protest, he rolled up his sleeves and helped out. I am satisfied, for now.

Courtesy of Wood-Mode Inc.

For my second book on kitchen design, I wanted to offer even more of what my readers are looking for— great photos! Here you will find over 350 images of to-die-for kitchens. Generously supplied by kitchen designers and top manufacturers, these pictures will allow you to peruse and pick your favorite styles of cabinets, floors, countertops, windows, and every other aspect of kitchen design from the comfort of, well, your own kitchen.

The trend toward bigger kitchens that open out into other parts of the home continues in the new millennium. Walls in older homes are being knocked out to allow people to be in two or three rooms at once—with visual access between living, dining, and cooking areas. New homes often incorporate a "great room" to serve the same purpose, and this book has lots of ideas about incorporating drop ceilings, islands, and floor surface changes to divvy up the space.

Speaking of which, islands—usually equipped with countertop seating—continue to be one of the most popular kitchen design elements. This is a wonderful trend that helps provide company, if not assistance, for the cook in the kitchen. To add to the attraction, more and more kitchens include a cabinet just for the television set. Some kitchen owners are going so far as to incorporate comfy upholstered chairs and sofas in the cooking domain.

Besides being the heart of the interior, kitchens are often the pathway to the exterior. They link up to sunrooms, decks, and patios for alfresco dining. And when the weather isn't cooperating, those inside often enjoy awesome views through bay windows and big glass doors.

Today's kitchen designs reflect our tremendous rise in spending power, as well as a new appreciation for quality materials. The images in this book portray a stunning array of fine tiles, woods, stone, brick, and glass—classic materials requiring fine craftsmanship for installations. And we can't forget the advances in more modern materials, like resilient flooring that mimics wood and may outdo the trees in terms of longevity and ease of upkeep.

These are dream kitchens, but everything in them is real and obtainable. A list of resources at the back will help you find the items found on these pages. The professional designers and suppliers listed herein would be more than happy to help you fit the look you like into the space you have. When it comes to the kitchen, there's no limit to what you can cook up.

SMALL SPACES

Today's new homes are being built to enormous scale, and the kitchen is part of this "growing" trend. But not everyone enjoys an enormous area in which to cook. Many people simply don't want to prepare elaborate meals, to spend hours in the kitchen.

Scaled down kitchens may be far more suitable for the bachelor, or the busy, working couple. If only one family member likes cooking, he or she may want a small space in which to perform—no one else is welcome.

Further, those who occupy older homes may be shopping for a facelift for their smaller kitchens.

This chapter offers big ideas for the little space. These go well beyond the traditional light colors and spare lines to open up a small room. In fact, many go right ahead and indulge in warm dark woods, flooring, and ceramic tiles, adding richness and texture to more concentrated spaces. There are great ideas for stretching countertops around corners and carrying cabinetry into adjacent rooms to create more space. Included too, are ideas for crossing the lines into eating or sitting areas to eke out a little more work/storage space for food.

Most importantly, these wonderful photos show that bigger isn't necessarily better—or more beautiful. This chapter offers opportunities to be lavish with what little you have. Indulge and enjoy!

Courtesy of Covenant Kitchens & Baths, Inc.

An air of grandeur is achieved with a sweeping arched entryway and a bold island work area. Behind is a bright swath of paneled windows. Every inch of white space is put to use here for storage or sterling white appliances. A double oven is tucked on one side of the archway and a wet bar on the other side to maximize the space of the kitchen.

A lot was made of a little space here, using cabinetry to create storage space from floor to ceiling, with a small ceiling cutout to add airiness.

Courtesy of Star Mark, Inc.

There's no work surface for the baker like wood, and here a big chunk of it offers space for kneading and cutting. An obvious wood lover, this homeowner filled the kitchen with southern pine cabinetry, complemented by rich red countertops and white appliances for contrast. By extending the cabinetry along a hallway, kitchen storage space was vastly increased.

Courtesy of Southern Pine Council

Naturally finished hickory cabinets extend around the corner to help the cook maximize her storage space in this small kitchen. Detailing on the range hood and an English country valance above a shelving unit add interest.

Courtesy of Aristokraft®

A small kitchen is spruced up with natural blonde cabinetry and a big arched window. Storage space extends around the outside walls.

Courtesy of Aristokraft®

A curved shelf over the island is a unique feature in this kitchen, extending the work space into an adjacent eating area. Other features for the compact kitchen include a handy built-in cutting board next to the sink and single-burner stove.

Courtesy of Brookhaven Cabinetry

An extra sink on the island allows helpers to pitch in with food preparation and clean-up chores. The double sink under the window is set up for the heavy duty work. Storage space has been maximized in this small kitchen with solid cabinetry on the walls and under the island.

Courtesy of Brookhaven Cabinetry

Staggered cabinet heights and a detailed valance on top add interest to this small kitchen area. As much as possible, this room was left open to adjacent living areas, while cabinets were designed to increase storage space. A ceramic range hood adds architectural interest, and an island helps to maximize workspace.

Photography by Keith Lanpher/Courtesy of Fisher Group

Courtesy of Kountry Kraft

An island work station creeps across the line between kitchen and dining areas to help expand the small space. Additional cabinetry in the island helps make possible the long countertop on the outside wall. Handmade tiles on the countertop, backsplash, and floor provide rustic accent to the simple cherry cabinets and smooth granite island countertop for this Colonial-style kitchen.

Even if you don't have a lot, you can make it pretty. Here a lovely Oriental rug, granite countertops, and a colorful tile backsplash add interest to a tiny space. An attractive pantry cabinet was added flush with the far wall, and capped with crown molding to set it off.

Photography by Greg Hadley/Courtesy of Fisher Group

A kitchen and laundry were gutted in order to start over again with this small kitchen. Matching arches on two doorways and an arched window tie together a space now expanded and brightened with white custom cabinetry. Recessed lighting distributes light evenly throughout.

Courtesy of Cross Interiors

A warm, gray and cocoa antique finish on this cabinetry provides the kitchen's unique charm. This room incorporates a wonderful tile backsplash over an expansive cooktop and an enormous farmer's sink. Nearby, an elegant, built-in china cabinet shows off a collection of glassware. A handy sink and wrap-around countertop lead to the dining area beyond.

Courtesy of Rutt of Atlanta

Photography by Keith Lanpher/Courtesy of Fisher Group

The texture and warmth of natural stone make this kitchenette exemplary. A smooth cooktop increases counter space when not in use. Shelves under the range hood free precious cabinet space for other uses. The contrast of stainless steel cooking equipment with stone and painted white cabinets creates an elegant, understated, but not too busy look for this small space.

Courtesy of Victoria Benatar Urban

In Manhattan, kitchen spaces are almost always very small. Here storage space was maximized. All appliances are American brands in black to match the new floors and countertop. Cherry wood cabinetry and light blue walls complete the elegant look. Under-cabinet lighting and a mirrored backsplash were added for drama.

Courtesy of Kountry Kraft

Arched cabinetry reaches up to draw attention to the lofty heights in this kitchen. Crisp white with black accents in the ceiling border, countertop, appliances, and flooring give this kitchen an orderly, cleanly atmosphere.

Modular cabinets and shelving are mostly for show in this kitchen.
It will be next to impossible to access the contents of drawers so
high up without a tall step ladder. Still, the look was worth it, paired
with a wine rack and plaids for an updated old-fashioned look.
Imitating stone, "Antiquity" luxury vinyl tile holds everything up.

Courtesy of Lori Engelhart

A lot was fit into this little kitchen, including the luxury of seating at the counter. Cabinets stretching up to the ceiling help create more storage, so the kitchen "works" too.

Simple lines, natural colors, and a variety of textures are well suited for this California-style kitchen. The clean lines of Sienna Maple cabinets stand in attractive contrast to the rough exposed stone walls.

Courtesy of Merillat Industries

A wonderful little wet bar was added around the corner from this kitchen, helping to tie in the outer dining area with matching cherry cabinetry and providing workspace for a helper.

Courtesy of IXL Cabinets

By combining dining and working areas, these homeowners were able to leave a wall open so that this small kitchen is connected with living areas. White cabinetry and walls allow a tile backsplash and granite counters to shine.

Courtesy of Blue Bell Kitchens

A wonderful symphony of varying countertop heights with lustrous natural-finish wood give this small kitchen character. Crystal knobs and lustrous white finish create an antique appearance for new cabinetry, and white finishes on the appliances allow them to blend in.

Courtesy of Blue Bell Kitchens

Courtesy of Cross Interiors

This little kitchen had to look good, had to match adjoining rooms that looked into it, and had to show off the antique pieces proudly collected by the owner. A new floor was custom cut and stained to tie into the existing floors in the eating area. Recessed and under-counter lighting was added. Hand-forged hinges on the cabinetry are a wonderful, custom addition.

A literary kitchen, this one quotes the Bard above the sink, and proudly displays cookbooks below the counter. "Cobblestone" tiles on the floor and mix-and-match finishes on the cabinetry create a unique, old-time character for this small space.

Courtesy of Summitville Tiles, Inc.

Setting wood flooring on the diagonal adds an illusion of width to this kitchen. Tall banks of classic gray-stain cabinetry were built against a backdrop of brick and mortar for a feeling of age and grace. The red of the bricks is mirrored in a kilim runner.

Courtesy of Distinctive Kitchen & Bath Interiors

SLEEK AND MODERN

Europe is going all-out on the paired down, minimalist modern look, but it has been slower to catch on in the States. In a new millennium, it seems only a few are looking for the futuristic. Here are some shining examples.

Courtesy of Victoria Benatar Urban

As in the states, Venezuelan families gather in the kitchen. For a young couple with three children in Caracas, Venezuela, this kitchen incorporates a banquette and TV area. The designer contrasted the colorful fabric of the banquette with white cabinetry and appliances and checkerboard floor.

Courtesy of Euro Kitchen & Bath

This kitchen is all business for the serious cook. Stainless steel, frosted glass, and granite give the space a sleek, utilitarian feel. Nearby, a warm wood table and wicker chairs offer an invitation to linger.

A cook's dream kitchen, this working space was designed with a huge, freestanding range with six burners, a griddle, and a char-grill barbeque, another cooktop and under-counter wine cooler in an adjacent work area, an oversize refrigerator/freezer, and two dishwashers. An interesting feature in this kitchen is the shiny black floor, which complements the graphite gray appliances and contrasts with natural wood finishes on kitchen chairs and cabinets.

Courtesy of Viking

Exotic art and accents characterize this kitchen, which veers from modern cabinetry to country dining furniture. "Festiva" resilient sheet flooring provides a traditional accent underfoot.

Courtesy of Congoleum Corp.

Designer Jean M. Buchen, CKD, mixed modern stainless steel with warm ceramic tiles and soft white cabinetry for a unique effect in this kitchen.

Courtesy of Kountry Kraft

Ebony and ivory team up for a stunning kitchen/dining area, with splashes of primary colors in a collection of glassware and a cheerful painting of culinary delights. Sleek painted wood cabinetry and seamless countertop create a contemporary atmosphere, softened by wood flooring.

Courtesy of Rutt of Atlanta

A generous layout, with a large bar area, provides an inviting place for friends and family to meet. Textured birch on multi-layered wood is a great combination to complement the contemporary architecture.

Courtesy of bulthap corporation

Courtesy of bulthap corporation

Courtesy of bulthap corporation

In addition to food, a cook can create and recreate her work space with these free-ranging kitchen elements. System 20 units were designed for mobility, functionality, and value, and fashioned for any setting, from an Art Nouveau building to a spacious contemporary loft.

Utilizing minimal space, a super-thin range allows for storage space below. The designer has also allowed for workspace behind the range, and storage in the cramped corner of a slanted roof.

Courtesy of Blue Bell Kitchens

Modern appliances and lighting, sleek wall cabinets, and an enormous central island/table work to create a cook's dream kitchen.

ADDING ANTIQUITY

A new millennium, and the rage is all old. It's as though, with all the new—the growth, the change—we're finding comfort in the stability of the past. Witness phenomena like *The Antiques Road Show* and Ebay, which have capitalized on a keen interest in history.

So antique finishes for brand new cabinetry in brand new homes are almost the norm. Spice drawers, which are never used for such, have been revived and are often displayed at such a height that they have no practical value. And cabinetry is being designed to look more like free-standing antique furniture, with pie-safe screens, imperfect glass window panes, and butcher-block counters. We're returning to the low-tech, high quality materials of the past, too—using stone, tile, and distressed wood floors for a feeling of authentic old architecture. We're even adding ceiling beams of hand-hewn wood.

The effect is wonderful. And no one is sacrificing convenience here. A brick fireplace may surround the most modern of ovens while genuine cherry paneling conceals a super-size 'fridge.

These are the best of times!

You feel as though you've stepped back in time in this kitchen created by Designer Jean M. Buchen, CKD. Antiqued green cabinetry contrasts with natural pine in the flooring and beaded panels. A modern oven and microwave are almost lost in the country kitchen ambiance.

Courtesy of Kountry Kraft

A mammoth kitchen was made more homey with beams that define a ceiling, but don't cut out light from windows two stories above or impede an impressive range hood from stretching the eye and the imagination north. A rich, antique blue finish on the cabinetry adds depth and warmth. A large central workstation is divided up into open and closed spaces to add interest. The island is moveable, though you'd want to invite a few friends over to help with the task.

Courtesy of Distinctive Kitchen & Bath Interiors

Courtesy of Rutt of Atlanta

Here's a space that can accommodate dark tones. The kitchen opens up to a two-story seating area with a bank of beautiful windows and glass doors for a flood of natural lighting by day. By night, recessed lighting in a lowered ceiling structure diffuses light evenly over work areas of rich, polished granite. The cabinetry was stained in wood tones to tie in with a wonderful wood-beamed ceiling, as well as an antiqued green that gives tall cabinets the effect of furniture, and matches molding and trim above and below the stained cabinets.

Courtesy of Congoleum Corp.

Rough finished wood, an old-fashioned paned window, and a stone fireplace give this cooking and dining area a log cabin feel, underlined by "Navara" resilient sheet flooring.

Timeless elegance is created in this kitchen with classic cabinetry punctuated by gleaming gold hardware, a marble mantel over the oven and range, and tile countertops. A ship's wheel creates a handy hanger for kitchen implements, and a lit wine rack makes finding the right vintage easy.

Courtesy of Aristokraft®

An assortment of antiques is displayed against green stucco and slate flooring. Practical hardwood cabinetry and seamless counters add modern convenience to the Southwestern atmosphere.

Courtesy of Aristokraft®

Courtesy of Aristokraft®

Courtesy of Congoleum Corp.

Here a taste for the unusual shows through, with vintage signage, raw pine framing, and a russet paint for the cabinetry. The simple country theme is carried through in imitation "American Pine" resilient wood plank flooring.

By filling two walls with cabinets, this small kitchen space is left open to living and dining areas beyond. An antique butcher block table adds character and workspace.

A gorgeous, earthy mix of lightly finished wood cabinetry, tile flooring, and brickwork were used for this kitchen's foundation. Accents like copper and wicker add to the rich texture and tone of the room.

Courtesy of Aristokraft®

Courtesy of Wellborn Cabinet, Inc.

A luxurious expanse between wall and ceiling is graced with natural cabinetry and big-paned windows. A ceramic tile floor completes the open-air environment.

Mixing and matching cabinetry creates an old-fashioned feel for this kitchen. Here beaded, natural-finish cabinets are juxtaposed with a special white unit complete with pie-safe screened cabinets, plus spice and looking-glass drawers.

Courtesy of Plain & Fancy

Free-standing cherry furniture creates a classic kitchen. The mix and match finishes, along with both clear and frosted glass inserts, modern lighting fixtures and appliances, make it seem as though this kitchen has been in use for decades.

Courtesy of YesterTec

Details make all the difference in this collection of stunning maple cabinets. Accents like woven wire door inserts, fluted chamfer panels, French scroll valances, and accent stains add interest and beauty.

Courtesy of Star Mark, Inc.

A casual, rustic kitchen combines mixed tiles and ceramic floor for a solid feel. Rich Chocolate trim sets off the Harvest finish on the cabinetry.

Courtesy of Merillat Industries

An interesting effect is created by placing one central blue unit in an expanse of white. It ties in beautifully with blue tile countertops and concludes that this kitchen was customized.

Courtesy of Plain & Fancy

Blue is a favorite for traditional and country interiors. Here Nantucket Blue pigmented stain allows the maple grain to show through. A natural wood stain on both counter and floors adds contrast.

Courtesy of Merillat Industries

Courtesy of Poulin Design Remodeling

In updating a 1970s kitchen, the cabinets were antiqued using a moss-green base with a brown glaze. Granite countertops, a tumbled marble backsplash, and stainless steel appliances complete the final look.

A combination of architectural details, light finishes, and summery colors results in a fresh, comfortable working and gathering space. White frost finish was used on cherry wood for the cabinets, paired with a painted latte finish in the cook center. Charming, countrified sliding baskets for storage are decorative as well as functional.

Courtesy of Plain & Fancy

The owners of Historic Graystone Inn of Wilmington, North Carolina, wanted their bed and breakfast's kitchen to provide cooking comfort for different chefs and catering companies while keeping the home's historic elegance. Designer Cynthia Sporre maintained an authentic "old" look in the long-narrow room by using three different door styles, two contrasting wood stains, two hardware designs, and varied cabinetry heights, with lots of horizontal surface area.

Courtesy of Kitchen Blueprints

In order to create a bigger kitchen for this old stone home, an addition was added in post and beam style. A period look was maintained with the rough-finished wood and antique finishes on furniture-like cabinetry. Big windows, modern plumbing, and state-of-the-art appliances were blended into their antique surroundings.

Courtesy of Restore 'N More/Barbara Herr

An original chamber-oven fireplace with plaster surround is mirrored in a like surround for the home's new cooking center. An island was added in period style, and stained to match original floorboards. Lighted, glass-paneled cabinetry and narrow floor cabinets were carried out into a hallway to increase storage space and present an opportunity to show off a collection of glassware.

Courtesy of Restore 'N More/Barbara Herr

Courtesy of Restore 'N More/Barbara Herr

This restoration project added modern amenities like track lighting to old beams. A new central island was given an old finish while multiplying the room's workspace and creating a new sink area. Plank flooring was lightly finished to maintain the room's integrity.

The homeowner in this historic house allowed an old, hand-hewn timber to take center stage in this kitchen, building light blue cabinetry around it. The cabinetry blends with a blue slate farmer sink and countertop, and contrasts with off-white bead board walls and trim.

Courtesy of Blue Bell Kitchens

COUNTRY CHARM

You can take the kitchen out of the country, but the country has a way of sticking with kitchens. Blue and white, natural wood, animal accents, gingham checks, and traditional pottery are enduring and endearing kitchen hallmarks. The look is free of pretension, seeking only to enchant.

Nevertheless, we seem to have overcome the beribboned geese and gingerbread bears that dominated the country decorating scene for far too long. Today's country is a little more sophisticated, incorporating antiques and high-quality textures such as real tile and stone that add class to down-home ambiance.

Bead-board cabinetry in an Heirloom finish lends a country flavor to this kitchen, with added sophistication in the form of a lit cutout in the four-legged island and full crown molding on the wall cabinets. The refrigerator was tied in to the color scheme with matching wood panels.

Courtesy of Wood-Mode Inc.

Courtesy of Congoleum Corp.

All eyes on the window— a space no one can ignore with such striking window treatment and fancy cabinet frames. "Marcrest" resilient sheet flooring underscores the excitement above.

Courtesy of American Woodmark

Hickory with a spice finish lends a warm, natural glow to this room. Designer Connie Edwards completed the natural order of things with terra-cotta tile, wicker, and rich, warm ceiling border wallpaper.

Courtesy of Wood-Mode Inc.

A beautiful wall cabinet with plate rack and glass panels dominates this kitchen, positioned above a mosaic tile backsplash. The central island unit is all business, with an antiqued green finish and seamless countertop.

A natural finish on the wood cabinetry paired with an artful assortment of tile makes this kitchen unique.

Courtesy of Aristokraft®

Photography by David Schilling/Courtesy of Jim Bishop Cabinets, Inc.

Courtesy of Wood-Mode Inc.

Duotone finish scheme combines pickle finish on the cabinet box and accessories, gray with chocolate on the doors and drawer fronts.

Curtains soften a built-in china cabinet with shallow drawers and a great collection of glass panels. Extensive molding stretches to the pressed-tin ceiling and circles the kitchen.

Old world charm is created with hand-hewn wood beams and warm wood finish on the cabinets. A unique chandelier with electric candle-fixtures fits right in.

Courtesy of Wood-Mode Inc.

This is a great kitchen for someone who loves to keep everything close at hand. Here the homeowner displays an eclectic assortment of antique kitchen ware, dried herbs, and colorful cooking ingredients. Open cabinetry is juxtaposed with plenty of drawers.

Courtesy of Aristokraft®

Here's a luxurious collection of cabinets for storage, with matching fronts for refrigerator, trash compactor, and dishwasher. The stove is neatly framed by a fancy range hood and tile backsplash, flanked by two high arching windows.

Courtesy of Wood-Mode Inc.

Blue and white, neat and tidy, this kitchen is pure country charm. Tile countertops mimic the wallpaper to complete the effect, which is softened ever so slightly by natural wood flooring and counters.

Courtesy of Wood-Mode Inc.

It would take a long time to peek in all these drawers! This kitchen is stacked with storage space, perfect for the orderly mind, and complete with some show-off shelving for a few collectible what-nots. Three separate work areas create wide open spaces for multi-cook families.

Courtesy of Wellborn Cabinet, Inc.

Here's a charming kitchen treatment. Natural-finish maple wall cabinetry was brought to the floor and staggered around an island for interesting effect. Cabinets on the left wall were set flush with paneling stained a light blue to blend with the countertop.

Courtesy of Wellborn Cabinet, Inc.

Green is a perennial favorite in the food place, and here it shines in the "Midnight" hues of do-it-yourself resilient tile, echoed in a sage countertop. Golden hues add complement, with natural finish on cabinetry and a subtle mushroom border tape.

Courtesy of Congoleum Corp.

In remodeling, portions of original cabinets were used with new door fronts and new "antique" hardware. A new garden window adds light, underlined by tiled backsplash and granite counter.

Courtesy of Cross Interiors

An expansive kitchen is made cozy with two-tone cabinetry, stone and granite countertops, and a textured tile backsplash. Nifty innovations here include a cutout area beside the sink for hanging wet hand towels. A bookshelf at the end of the island workstation marks the transition from food to family, tile to wood. Handmade valances finish all the open cabinets with a French touch.

Photography by Greg Hadley/Courtesy of Fisher Group

Photos by Jim Fiora/Courtesy of Covenant Kitchens & Baths, Inc.

Soft tones and a charming accents on the counter-to-ceiling tile backsplash give this room a homey, country appeal.

Photography by Keith Lanpher/Courtesy of Fisher Group

Layers of charm were added to this homey kitchen, with plaid curtains, collectibles, and Oriental carpets, set against a backdrop of multi-tone cabinetry and countertop. Several different cabinet finishes provide interest. The effect is a new kitchen that looks timeless.

Photography by Keith Lanpher/Courtesy of Fisher Group

Kitchen transitions to dining area with a darker finish on the cabinetry to match the dining set. Pretty details like hand-painted tiles on a custom range hood and a leaded-glass insert on the corner cabinet add beauty. A chest of drawers dividing the room is really a portable island. It has casters, an electrical outlet, and leaves on each side that can fold up when the homeowner needs additional space.

Courtesy of Cross Interiors

Using angles and soft radius, this square room was transformed into an architectural delight. The boomerang island, topped with granite, visually expands the room, along with a new bay area using French doors as windows. New brick was stained and sealed to create a warm, old effect and laid on the diagonal. New white lacquered cabinets and hand-painted tile countertops create a crisp, transitional look.

The old growth timber appearance of new flooring adds authenticity to this restored new England home, and expands the small kitchenette into the dining area.

Courtesy of Forest Floors Inc.

A cutout adds architectural interest and allows the cook to enjoy her guests in the adjacent dining area, as well as the view. The floor may be deceiving—it is resilient sheet flooring named "Woodland."

Courtesy of Congoleum Corp.

Photography by Keith Lanpher/Courtesy of Fisher Group

This kitchen was kept proportional, occupying a corner that explodes into a soaring roof line and opening on to dining and living areas of the home. Designer Peggy Fisher created interest in two-tones of cabinetry and a seamless green countertop, tied together by a decorative tile backsplash. A collection of early twentieth century antiques in the rest of the house are perfectly at home with the Craftsman detailing and glass mullions.

Courtesy of Poulin Design Remodeling

The couple who requested a remodel were interviewed extensively about how they would contribute to the food preparation process and interact with each other. The result is separate counter spaces, cooking areas, sinks, and storage. Common ovens and waste containment are accessed by wide corridors around a central working area with adjacent seating. Simple cherry wood cabinets are embraced by the soft plastered white of the surrounding walls.

Courtesy of Southern Pine Council

Courtesy of Star Mark, Inc.

A showpiece tops the sink, with display shelf and fancy appliqué above, underlined by spice drawers. Tile backsplash and seamless counter make for a low-maintenance kitchen.

Wood on white dominates this country style kitchen. Unique, open compartments on the upper cabinets and the side of the island create display space.

The basic colors of ceiling trim tiles play out in accent pieces against a backdrop of solid maple cabinets in natural finish.

Courtesy of Merillat Industries

A variety of finishes on new cabinetry gives the impression of authentic age-old furniture in this remodeling job. A refrigerator was paneled to keep the appliance unobtrusive, and a wall was removed to create space for a large island and adjacent eating area. A ceiling richly hung with copper and wicker kitchen implements carries country charm from one room into the next.

Courtesy of Restore 'N More/Barbara Herr

Decorative tile trim around the countertops and sparks of accent tiles on the backsplash adorn this kitchen. The tile theme was carried up to the drop ceiling with recessed lighting. A soft, neutral tile floor and rich wood stain lend contrast.

Courtesy of Summitville Tiles, Inc.

A window is allowed to dominate this room, with the barest of reed coverings, and two matching wicker chairs paying it homage. By day you might overlook the expansive island with built-in storage. Its counterparts on the wall were topped with beaded board and molding to create an antique/country effect.

Courtesy of Blue Bell Kitchens

OPENING TO THE OUTSIDE

There are those among us who only wash the garden dirt off our hands and come inside because we're hungry. When it takes too long to cook up the grub, we get downright starved for the out of doors.

These days, improved technology and craftsmanship make it possible to create a wall of glass without cooking everyone inside during the summer or heating the great wild yonder during the winter.

This means that, come hail or high water, we're sitting inside and looking out at it all with smiles on our faces. It also means we can grow oxygen-producing plants inside, as well as some delicious fresh herbs. And we get all that yummy light.

So here, for the claustrophobic-at-heart, is a mouth-watering selection of bright indoor designs for those who can't bear to be inside.

A giant, arched window in a painted brick wall dominates this kitchen, and was left to shine through the sheerest of curtains. A scanty underlining of antique-gray finished cabinets ties in with the rest of the kitchen.

Courtesy of Wood-Mode Inc.

With scenery like this, you don't want to miss an inch of it. Cabinets were doubled up on a back wall and under the counter to keep a clean sweep view of this wooded hillside. Skylights multiply the natural light available by day.

Courtesy of Lori Engelhart

A pottery sun mask dominates this kitchen, with a collection of small candles underneath for nighttime. A natural wash stain on the cabinets allows other elements to shine, like fancy glass fronts on cabinets over the wonderful black farmer's sink with golden fixtures.

Courtesy of Wood-Mode Inc.

Courtesy of Cross Interiors

To create the sophisticated country kitchen desired by the owner, this project began by gutting the former kitchen and eating area. Lack of light was a major issue to be addressed, and was corrected by installing a greenhouse window. The old fluorescent lighting system in the ceiling was replaced with new lighting under the cabinets and low-voltage lighting in the crown molding to enhance the feeling of space. The wood floor was refurbished and complemented by butcher-block counters and contrasting white cabinets.

This addition more than doubled the kitchen. The island houses a sink, garbage disposal, cook top, and down draft system, and a large oven under the counter. A dishwasher and recycle center, along with another garbage disposal, are housed under the counter. The light fixtures in the kitchen and dining areas were custom designed by Cheryl Casey Ross, who also designed the other wrought iron work in the room. The chef's pantry was windowless, so one was painted, and open custom cabinets were added to create plenty of storage.

Courtesy of Cross Interiors

Courtesy of Rutt of Atlanta

The walls were cleared for this kitchen to allow big open windows, free of any obstruction, as well as an attractive corner stove top and range hood with tile wall treatment. Storage was maximized below the countertops, and an attractive island houses a big farmer's sink, a dishwasher, and trash compactor, and also provides a gracefully curved seating area. A nearby buffet area contains a ready indoor grill.

Courtesy of Four Season Sunrooms

Let the sun shine in. A narrow kitchen grew up here with the addition of overhead glass panels. This allows an outside wall to accommodate a lot more cabinets without sacrificing any room for windows, and without creating claustrophobia. The adjacent dining area features insulated glass all the way to the floor for maximum light and visual vantage.

A sweeping arch of windows adds luxurious space and light to this kitchen. A serving buffet is placed to advantage for both cook, working off to the left, and guests.

Courtesy of Weather Shield Windows & Doors

Lots of white and big windows add up to bright. The subtle door style of the cabinets mimics the window panes beyond. Staggered floor tiles create a patio feel underfoot.

Courtesy of Star Mark, Inc.

Blonde cabinetry and wood flooring create a soft backdrop for dramatic black-and-white backsplash and striped wallpaper. A moveable center island table creates a convenient workspace and an option when more space is needed.

Courtesy of Fieldstone Cabinetry, Inc.

A picture window incorporates a few decorative panes that mimic the glass-front cabinets, but minimize interruption of the outside view.

Courtesy of Weather Shield Windows & Doors

Courtesy of Four Season Sunrooms

Kitchens are quickly extended by shifting the dining area out-of-doors. Here solariums allow the cook a wide vista, the family an all-season alfresco dining experience, and even a little office space.

Solid oak cabinetry and window frames add warmth to a snazzy checkerboard floor, black countertop, and stainless steel appliances. Windows by the main work area add appeal to chores.

Courtesy of Weather Shield Windows & Doors

Open windows and open cabinetry equal a bright, comfortable kitchen. A natural stain on the cabinetry and wood ceiling and floors lend an earthy air to the room, obviously designed for someone who doesn't want to be too far from the outdoors.

Courtesy of Weather Shield Windows & Doors

Window treatment has been minimized, in order to maximize sunlight and view. Tall wall cabinets create a sense of vertical space. The maple cabinetry is complemented by a hardwood floor. A bump-out sink base is framed with fluted, chamfered columns that lend elegance and flair.

Courtesy of Star Mark, Inc.

Courtesy of Congoleum Corp.

Well chosen, the taupe walls set off sparkly cabinetry, as do the neutral "tiles" of "Courtland" resilient sheet flooring.

Here's a home for wood lovers, with wood paneling, cabinetry, and floor. For contrast, soapstone countertops and an antiqued central island were added. Though they look smart, the stools pulled up to the island won't allow a body to dine there. These are for perching only.

Courtesy of Blue Bell Kitchens

This spacious kitchen was designed by Cynthia Sporre to accommodate some serious cooking, with state-of-the-art appliances, two wet sinks, pots and pans at the ready, and acres of counter space. However, it's not totally focused on the work at hand. Natural light and window space have been maximized here, with panes stretching under cabinets along the outside wall and curtains cut from the equation. Instead, window treatments were placed up above, with a bold slash of black and white.

Courtesy of Kitchen Blueprints

Courtesy of Congoleum Corp.

This kitchen uses texture in wallpaper, plants, and accent pieces like the wine rack with wicker to subtly lull the senses. There's no view that isn't pleasing, and none that screams for attention, right down to the "Shalestone" luxury vinyl tile.

Neoclassical and European

In a golden age it's only natural that designers and homeowners reflect back on another zenith in the history of design and architecture. The aesthetics of our Greek and Roman forebears, as well as our rich European roots, are filtering into contemporary kitchens. The effects are, simply, stunning.

Polished marble is used generously in this kitchen, on countertop, island, and an inlaid kitchen table. The cabinetry has neo-classic detailing, and faux stone effects in the baseboard. Even the ceiling has been pitched to create an illusion of classic Roman architecture, and the refrigerator has been paneled to resemble columns.

Courtesy of Distinctive Kitchen & Bath Interiors

Courtesy of Schenck and Company Fine Wood Floors

Wide, hand-distressed mesquite plank flooring and a vaulted brick ceiling trace the length of this long kitchen, making the narrow dimensions classic. A statue standing in the window takes center stage.

Mixing quartersawn white oak and lacewood with pink marble takes both talent and technology as the different densities expand and contract differently in response to temperature changes. The parquet blocks were hand cut prior to installation. This is a kitchen in which no detail was spared, from the ram's-head legs on the island work station to the elaborately carved range hood.

Courtesy of John's Custom Floors, Inc.

Here's an interesting contrast between the natural finish of wall cabinetry and the blacks and steely grays of a central island work station. Dark granite countertops tie the look together.

Courtesy of Rutt of Atlanta

Details add elegance to this softly toned kitchen. Over-glazed, decorative tiles take center stage, while twisted-rope molding and spiraled columns tie the room together. Lime-stone was used for the counter and floor.

Courtesy of Euro Kitchen & Bath

Warm honey tones, with a rich custom handmold tile range hood and luxurious window treatments dominate this kitchen. Carved details on the chairs, island, and crown molding add opulence, along with granite and Corian® countertops and ceramic tile on the floor.

Courtesy of Kitchens Unique

An enormous, arched window commands attention—and island seating is poised to enjoy it. Likewise, a cook at the stove can keep an eye on the neighborhood. Underfoot, a floral motif adorns resilient sheet flooring, and a wrought-iron rack holds a collection of copper and terra-cotta.

Courtesy of Congoleum Corp.

Courtesy of Crossville Porcelain Stone/USA

The designers had fun here, playing with seven tile colors to create a diamond-pattern floor mosaic, interrupted by another pattern under the kitchen table. A scalloped Corian countertop is another impressive artistic flourish by New York designers John Buscarello and Maggi Cohen. A gorgeous fireplace with gas log and a built-in entertainment center make this the family hangout.

A rich dark finish and classic crowning features on the cabinetry lend a distinctive air to this kitchen. A wraparound counter makes the most of a small inner work area.

Courtesy of Wood-Mode Inc.

Small details—a beautiful wallpaper above the wall cabinets, a handsome tile backsplash— decorate this kitchen. The whole is held together by a light, natural-looking finish on the cabinetry with classic detailing including display shelves, leaded glass windows, and a wine rack.

Courtesy of Wood-Mode Inc.

Angles and height add interest to this kitchen, and a brick surround and heavy crown molding add class. A rich finish on the maple cabinetry and polished granite countertops complete the rich atmosphere in this stately room.

Courtesy of Covenant Kitchens & Baths, Inc.

Natural wood finish paired with genuine ceramic tiles give this kitchen its golden glow. Slate-colored tiles on the backsplash tie the look in with stainless steel appliances for state-of-the-art efficiency.

Courtesy of Laufen International Ceramic Tile

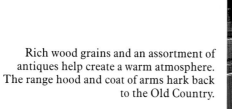

Rich wood grains and an assortment of antiques help create a warm atmosphere. The range hood and coat of arms hark back to the Old Country.

Courtesy of Aristokraft®

Courtesy of Congoleum Corp.

Courtesy of Congoleum Corp.

Architectural details such as the columns supporting the island seating counter and the archway to outside doors add grace to this spacious kitchen. The cabinetry is allowed to shine against patterned wallpaper and "Mosaic Surround" luxury vinyl tile.

"Hand-painted" tiles on the walls are repeated in wrought iron, for a French bistro effect. The outdoor cafe charm is completed by "Onyx" resilient sheet flooring.

A chocolate glaze on maple provides an antique charm to clean new cabinetry. Against the wall, fancy details create a symmetrical unit surrounding the stove, and a silhouette cutout in the island houses a collection of shiny metal kitchenware.

Courtesy of Fieldstone Cabinetry, Inc.

Courtesy of Cross Interiors

Custom pine cabinetry and wood flooring give this country kitchen its warm feeling, complemented by linens and accessories in the bright blues and yellows of Provence. The kitchen works beautifully for the large catered parties given by the homeowner, with expanses of counter space, double workstations, and an eye toward easy traffic flow. The granite island features a full-size sink, water filtration system, dishwasher, and disposal, and was designed for cleanup in the cooking area. The main sink area in front of a bay window is designed for general cleanup, located next to another dishwasher as well as the dish storage cabinets. Wine storage faces the dining room for easy access, and presents a nice view.

A high chair at a tall counter is an invitation to linger and gossip, overlooked by a soft lighting fixture. Classic molding atop solid cherry cabinetry lends a dignified air to the proceedings.

Courtesy of Fieldstone Cabinetry, Inc.

A brick surround over double, arched-front open cabinets simulates a fireplace, while repeating squares in the cabinetry and fanciful tile work create a rich room.

Courtesy of Wood-Mode Inc.

A brick backsplash creates the "hearth" of the home, framed by duo-toned cabinets—one set finished in oatmeal and glazed with chocolate, the other in a hunter green. Stucco walls complete the old-world feel.

Courtesy of Merillat Industries

This kitchen gains grace and distinction from cabinet detailing, with turned legs for a furniture effect, and deeply etched cabinet doors. A tile backsplash behind the range houses one of this kitchen's conveniences—a high faucet for filling big pots and providing a splash when needed.

Courtesy of Blue Bell Kitchens

Not Afraid of Color

There probably is some official psychological term for this, and the problem is definitely widespread. We all figure that we'll have to sell someday, and our favorite color certainly wouldn't be appropriate. So we're all living in eggshell-white homes. When someone does have the guts to slap some pink or purple on a wall, I think it deserves a resounding cheer. So here are a few fine examples of rainbow gusto. Some encouragement for the next wave of pioneers . . .

Who would have thought of a lavender ceiling? It's a lovely effect, paired with decorative border paper and fabrics and a blue counter and backsplash. Natural maple flooring and cabinetry provide contrast and continuity.

Courtesy of Dutch Made Custom Cabinetry Inc.

This kitchen is highlighted by fanciful touches of blue in the window frame, tile backsplash, and cabinet molding.

Courtesy of Wood-Mode Inc.

A coastal look is created by combining the rich tones of maple wood with honey glaze and shades of green and violet. High ceilings and stacked cabinets give a vertical feel to this kitchen. The island back features a bookcase for display and storage is accented with bead board panels. Open shelves on each side of the cook top provide easy access to potholders or spices.

Courtesy of Wellborn Cabinet, Inc.

A kitchenette is made memorable with two-tone cabinetry featuring red and gray base coats with chocolate glaze. Gray tiles key in with cabinet colors, and texture is added with stucco walls.

Photography by David Schilling/Courtesy of Jim Bishop Cabinets, Inc.

Courtesy of Wood-Mode Inc.

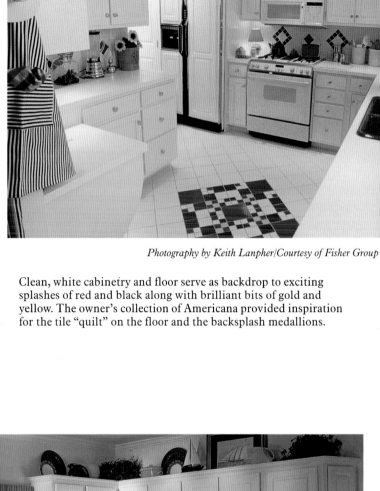

Photography by Keith Lanpher/Courtesy of Fisher Group

Clean, white cabinetry and floor serve as backdrop to exciting splashes of red and black along with brilliant bits of gold and yellow. The owner's collection of Americana provided inspiration for the tile "quilt" on the floor and the backsplash medallions.

Molding is used to create a beamed effect in the ceiling, tying in with white cabinetry below. Yellow walls and a crimson central island add striking spot color.

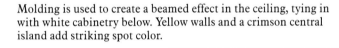

A small kitchen is expanded with bright, white cabinetry in sleek "Augusta" style, to maximize storage space. A collection of bright ceramics adds color atop white marble counters and on the upper crust of full overlay molding.

Courtesy of Aristokraft®

A small kitchen gets a warm golden glow, from the copper pots and plant filtered sunlight, to a faux "Royal Cherry" laminate floor. Jade green dominates in the countertops, tile, cabinetry, and trim.

Courtesy of Congoleum Corp.

Assorted finishes on the cabinetry create a playful effect in this kitchen, mimicked in the tile countertop of the island. The wood tones are framed by a rich red on the walls.

Photography by David Schilling/Courtesy of Jim Bishop Cabinets, Inc.

Courtesy of Plain & Fancy

Evoking blue skies and big water, bright blue cabinetry is the signature of the "casual coastal" look. Stainless steel appliances and pressed tin backsplash complete the cool effect. Distinctive, diamond-shaped mullions in the glass-front cabinet are echoed in a wine rack, flanked by a wine refrigeration unit and spice drawers.

Courtesy of Summitville Tiles, Inc.

What a cheerful room, covered with fanciful tiles with edibles, animals, and flowers, plus the names of family members sprinkled along countertops and backsplash.

Red grout between black tiles creates dramatic effect in this kitchen, complemented by glass-fronted cabinetry stained a rich cherry, plus black appliances.

Courtesy of Summitville Tiles, Inc.

Decorative tiles adorn this kitchen, including two murals in porcelain behind the stove and on a work-area backsplash.

Courtesy of Summitville Tiles, Inc.

Courtesy of Hanford Cabinet & Woodworking

Designed for a remodeled barn, this kitchen is an unabashed barn red, right down to the tiles on the floor. The cabinetry maintains a rustic styling with turned legs and solid wood knobs, set against a backdrop of contrasting white bead board. Original ceiling timbers are outfitted with modern lights. The refrigerator is concealed behind door-style panels.

Formal Impressions

Some kitchens have an air, a grace, a distinction that knocks you back at first sight and evokes a reverential "wow." These are places of grandeur. Halls of great cooking. Impressive spaces that speak of taste and wealth.

This impression is often gained with darker wood stains, heavy crown molding, gleaming gold hardware, and lots of glass-fronted cabinetry lit and sparkly with formal crystal. Of course, soaring ceilings and monstrous room size don't hurt, either, if you want to make a big impression.

A small wet sink was set in cabinets that were made to imitate a massive buffet/china cabinet. This pairs up neatly with a nearby desk work area and two wall cabinets flanking the stove. The island also gets an antique furniture effect, with turned-wood legs for illusion.

Courtesy of Wood-Mode Inc.

The color scheme has been reversed from the norm here for a crisp, orderly effect, with wood-stain walls contrasted against clean white cabinetry. The result is a stunning stage for work and eating spaces. Fluted molding and furniture-style legs under the sink add interest. China storage has been married to a small office area, making this a very useful corner.

Courtesy of Covenant Kitchens & Baths, Inc.

Courtesy of Cross Interiors

A crackle finish was added to cabinetry in need of a facelift here, along with custom-made knobs of Star-fire glass. The same glass was used over the buffet, where panels were removed to create lighted cabinets and add depth to the room. Mirrors were added to the backsplash in the U-shaped sink area to help expand the room. The mirrors were etched from the back to reflect the grapes and leaf motif found in the custom-designed wine rack.

This remodeling job stayed true to the home's original 1920s design, yet added modern convenience and storage. A gray base coat and chocolate glaze add antique character to the cabinetry and harmonize with polished granite countertops and stainless steel appliances. A wood floor was refinished for stunning effect.

Photography by David Schilling/Courtesy of Jim Bishop Cabinets, Inc.

Free of hardware, the flat faces of the classically finished cabinets lend a formal air to the room. Organized and lit, two end cabinets create a stunning entryway.

Courtesy of Brookhaven Cabinetry

A wood lover designed this brand-new kitchen in a brand new house, from the custom country oak plank flooring to the natural-looking finish of the cabinetry.

Courtesy of Forest Floors Inc.

This kitchen has several features that set it apart from the norm. Designer Dee Hurst-Funk, CKD, added elegance with a contrasting corner cabinet unit mimicking an elaborate china cabinet. A glass showcase separates the kitchen from a small window seat, and an overhead lighting unit coordinates with the rich red finish of the cabinets.

Courtesy of Kountry Kraft

This kitchen corners into an office area, with a built-in round table set to make the transition. Cabinetry and countertop tie it all together, with the same look for the

cook's storage and display case china cabinets, the office supplies, and the adjacent wet bar. A stainless steel cooking area is the hallmark of a true cook.

Courtesy of Rutt of Atlanta

Long and lean wall cabinets get additional dignity from generous crown molding, carved details, and an antique finish. A ceramic tile backsplash adds warmth, as does an antique green finish on center island cabinetry.

Floor to ceiling cabinets make the most of a small kitchen, and allow for the luxury of a cutout window to a family room. An overhang of the marble countertop creates an attractive seating area.

Courtesy of Distinctive Kitchen & Bath Interiors

Courtesy of Rutt of Atlanta

A post and beam room gets elegant underpinnings with soft-finished classically-styled cabinetry and a big, granite-topped island workstation and table in antique green. The family dining area beyond is decorated in a manner keeping with this home's colonial atmosphere.

A rich burgundy finish on the woodwork and earthen tile tones create a formal atmosphere in this kitchen, completed by carved rope in the classic crown molding, raised panel doors on the cabinets, and bright brass hardware.

Courtesy of Fieldstone Cabinetry, Inc.

Matching door panels integrate a refrigerator into the overall kitchen, here in a solid surround of fine cherry cabinetry.

Courtesy of Fieldstone Cabinetry, Inc.

Rich cherry cabinetry with matching refrigerator panels and bar stools make this a cozy kitchen. A large picture window floods the space with light, and lighting under the cabinets fills in when the sun goes down.

Courtesy of Fieldstone Cabinetry, Inc.

Photos by Jim Fiora/Courtesy of Covenant Kitchens & Baths, Inc.

The arched molding above the oven and range are mirrored in a nearby buffet unit. Classic molding is key to this kitchen's elegance, underscored by wood countertop and floor. The central island unit has a gracefully carved edge, and the solid base is finished in an antique gray.

Photos by Jim Fiora/Courtesy of Covenant Kitchens & Baths, Inc.

Fido wasn't forgotten when this kitchen was designed, with his own special drawers incorporated into the cabinetry. The kitchen's cream and green color theme was carried over into the adjacent dining area.

Courtesy of Merillat Industries

Courtesy of Fieldstone Cabinetry, Inc.

Rich color is paired with traditional styling details for elegant effect. The island serves as additional countertop workspace, a place to display collectibles, and also as an eating/buffet area. Underneath the cooktop, a configuration of four drawers flanked by a vertical arrangement of spice drawers sets off that area of the kitchen.

A dream kitchen for the cook who needs a lot of counter space, this room provides plenty of room to work as well as under-counter storage areas. Up above, open cabinets create display space for favorite china pieces.

Shaker-inspired lines were used in this cabinet door style, providing a stunning foundation for the elegant black, solid-surface countertops, stainless steel appliances, and chrome knobs and fixtures. Designed for the serious cook, this kitchen has double range and ovens, a handy island preparation center with bar sink, and ample countertop and storage areas.

Courtesy of Fieldstone Cabinetry, Inc.

Courtesy of Rutt of Atlanta

A brick wall, granite counters, and hardwood flooring and cabinetry combine for a solid, conventional kitchen. There are some nice touches here that make this kitchen user friendly, such as the stainless steel racks for cooking oils and spices over the stove, and the blackboard panels on the refrigerator that create a family communication center.

Classic crown molding on cherry cabinets give this room a distinctive air, coupled with clean white countertops and appliances. The chair in the foreground shows that this kitchen was integrated with the family's living space.

Courtesy of Yorktown Cabinets

Formal touches in the wallpaper pattern, white china, and the high-back chairs at the counter add a posh touch to a gentle, country-style kitchen.

Courtesy of IXL Cabinets

A cathedral ceiling adds air and elegance to this room, accommodating a tall picture window trimmed with a valance that keys in to the top of the cabinetry. A rich wood finish and soapstone countertops give this room its stately appeal.

Courtesy of Blue Bell Kitchens

Courtesy of Barbara Herr

A long, narrow kitchen was maximized during this remodeling job. White cabinetry helps to expand the room, anchored by granite countertops and tile floors. Refitted antique lighting units maintain the historic character of the home. A carved wooden chest was topped with granite to serve as a moveable island. The cabinetry under the windows was kept narrow, allowing an overhang of the counter so that the space can be used for both seating and working.

Courtesy of Barbara Herr

Wonderful extras—fancy crown molding, corner supports on the island, scalloped edging on the countertop, inset tile on tile on the backsplash—give this kitchen distinction.

GATHERING PLACES

These days, this is what a kitchen is all about—hanging out together near the food source. It used to be that you'd leave the house when it got too hot out and go to a whole separate building to cook. If you had money, you paid someone to cook for you in a room set well off from the areas where the family and guests congregated and ate. And, of course, cooking was what Mom did, single-handedly.

Cooking was a lonely endeavor.

No more. Now there's plenty of counter space, and often extra sinks so everyone can pitch in and help out. There are chairs in the kitchen now, so people can pull a stool up to the counter and keep you company while you do the work. Sometimes there's even a comfy seating area close by. Desks are often included so that someone can work on paying the bills while dinner is underway. And TVs are becoming increasingly common kitchen fixtures as the family finds that, more and more often, this is the room that they're in.

Pull up a chair: this island seating provides the perfect audience for a cook who loves her work. The high ceiling in her theater is downplayed, while underfoot is an earthy clay-colored stage of "Brookfield" resilient sheet flooring.

Courtesy of Congoleum Corp.

Angled islands bring the family in closer while leaving loads of workspace for the cook. A diamond-pattern tile backsplash dominates the room, framed by white cabinetry.

Courtesy of Brookhaven Cabinetry

A shoulder-height shelf supports a few colorful objects and underlines two windows in a seating area. The dark tones of the wood trim are complemented in "Courtyard" resilient sheet flooring.

Courtesy of Congoleum Corp.

Courtesy of Congoleum Corp.

A ceiling is made to seem higher with a few clever touches—beams up above and a matching shelf over the range dividing an expansive tile backsplash. The central wall tiles reflect the terra cotta-colored "Santa Fe" resilient flooring. Out of the cook's way, there is an office area and a wet bar to satisfy different needs.

Courtesy of Lori Engelhart

A large island creates space for spectators and kitchen socialites while keeping them out of the cook's way. If the cook isn't on center stage, the television is, occupying a neat little corner cabinet space. Another focal point is the garden window with built-in plant shelf, allowing the cook a full view of the backyard.

Traditional, clean, and comfortable, this is a working kitchen with room for everyone to pitch in on the effort of meal preparation. A wine rack and counter area create a gathering place and additional storage space.

Courtesy of Lori Engelhart

Warm earth tones and soft lighting in the ceiling and under cabinets create a comfort zone in this kitchen. The floor here is particularly intriguing, with variations in the pattern around the island and in the hallway beyond. A marble countertop with raised bar on the island creates an attractive party spot, with more seating just beyond at a table.

Courtesy of Distinctive Kitchen & Bath Interiors

Once a long narrow kitchen, this room was transformed into an open yet cozy work space with the introduction of angles. The extended snack bar encroaching slightly into the adjacent living space not only provides seating for the family, it creates the illusion of additional width within the space. An added bonus was a built-in pantry added on the back wall behind the oven.

Courtesy of Lori Engelhart

Lots of natural lighting and space make for a friendly, inviting place. Cabinets on the island back provide dish storage for the kitchen and snack bar while keeping the cook's view to the backyard and the family room.

Courtesy of Lori Engelhart

Photography by Keith Lanpher/Courtesy of Fisher Group

Kitchen and family dining area revolve around windows here, with an island work station and the bench both bowing toward the light. Floor tiles tie together the natural wood finishes with accent cabinets, black appliances, and a stone farmer's sink. A punched tin door front on the cabinet by the sink ventilates the compost bucket, which is accessed by a cover on the countertop for ease of use.

This kitchen is rich in workspace, with seemingly endless expanses of white countertop and a king's ransom in storage space, too. Natural wood tones carry the continuity of this lavishly squared off kitchen space.

Courtesy of Lori Engelhart

Courtesy of Lori Engelhart

This half-height, radiused wall provides snack bar seating while hiding the cooktop and countertop workspace from the adjacent diners. The emerald-green countertops provide continuity from the kitchen through the box bay window overlooking the Mississippi River.

Green walls and countertop provide counterpoint to lovely alder wood cabinetry. An overhang on one countertop provides a seated vantage point, made all the more attractive by two lovely wicker chairs.

Another room was incorporated in this remodeled kitchen job, and a large bay window and French doors were welcome additions for more light. The client requested an island with seating, as well as lots of counter space.

Courtesy of Cross Interiors

Courtesy of Restore 'N More/Barbara Herr

This family got a whole new center for socializing with this addition. One whole side was banked with windows, and another wall of cabinetry got glass fronts to mirror the look. Soft seating adjacent to the food preparation area as well as stools for helpers at the island ensure a steady supply of company for the cook.

An original, outside stone wall forms the focal point of this massive kitchen addition. The new room features beaded board ceiling panels with recessed lighting, oversize stone tiles for the floor, two great walls of windows, and antique finish on the cabinetry.

Courtesy of Restore 'N More/Barbara Herr

SHOWING OFF COLLECTIONS

Kitchens have always been prime spots for displaying and using wonderful old pottery and porcelain, basketry, and assorted tools and statuary. Here are some ample kitchens built with display in mind. Glass-fronted cabinetry and open shelves have been incorporated, allowing the owner to exhibit favorite bits and pieces gleaned at antique stores, auctions, and flea markets—or better yet, passed down through generations of the family.

Courtesy of Wood-Mode Inc.

An open island with glass-fronted display shelves dominates this kitchen, framed above by a mantel over the stove and display cabinets beside the sink. A completely modern kitchen that manages to look old in scale and appointments.

This cozy kitchen draws its character from patterned wallpaper, rich, classic wood cabinetry, and a merry blue countertop—a perfect setting for the owner's pottery collection.

Courtesy of Aristokraft®

A stunning expanse of blonde cabinetry is decorated with an inlay of decorative tile below the molding, and contrasted with granite countertops and the red earthen tones of a tile floor.

Courtesy of Summitville Tiles, Inc.

This kitchen work area centers around a range topped by a fret wood hood, a matching arch fret valance on the range base cabinet, and a square unit hanging over the island work area that holds antique pots and implements. Country table legs around the base cabinets, finished in Antique Evergreen, create the look of true furniture for the cabinetry.

Courtesy of Wellborn Cabinet, Inc.

Glorious space, rich with countertop and cabinetry, make this a cook's heaven. Glass-paneled showcases and polished marble surfaces give the owner bragging rights.

Courtesy of Kountry Kraft

Lots of lovely window panes in the windows, wall cabinets, and work station create a light feeling in this white kitchen. A wonderful wood counter on the island lends itself to baking chores.

Courtesy of American Woodmark

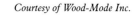

Courtesy of Wood-Mode Inc.

Decoration and function meet in natural maple cabinetry with raised panel doors topped by crown molding and set off with window panes, a spice shelf, and open display areas.

This kitchen literally sparkles with spotlights and a wall of picture-window cabinets.

Generous proportions allow plenty of space for showing off, here with glass-fronted cabinetry to showcase special porcelain pieces.

Here's a kitchen for the proud porcelain owner, with show windows for a neatly displayed collection. A blue stain gives these cabinets their unique style. Warm natural wood tones in the resilient flooring provide a homey feel.

A big chunk of island, angled, curved, and adorned with faux legs, display shelves, and a marble countertop, turns this small kitchen into a showplace while connecting it with outer living areas. An additional display cabinet and shelf work with the island to show off a porcelain collection.

Courtesy of Distinctive Kitchen & Bath Interiors

Courtesy of Distinctive Kitchen & Bath Interiors

Stacking cabinets at different heights creates intrigue, with additional contrast between classic crown molding and an arched window. Windowed cabinetry in the island creates a dramatic focal point.

Courtesy of Merillat Industries

Sparkling cabinets have the crisp, clean look that makes white a perennial favorite for use in the kitchen. Here crown molding and countertop edging team up for an elegant cabinet effect against blues, with a leaded picture window added for elegance.

Courtesy of Star Mark, Inc.

With the addition of pantry-size cabinets along the far wall, this kitchen accommodates an enormous amount of storage, yet allows the luxury of a long, low island for seating, socializing, and the outward vantage of a cook.

Courtesy of Wood-Mode Inc.

Stained bead board provides background here for white cabinetry topped by a pink countertop and farmer's sink.

A classic look for this bar area is created by shallow wall and floor cabinets, topped by a seamless black counter and enhanced all around by glass showcase windows.

Courtesy of Wood-Mode Inc.

FEMININE TOUCH

In the average household, it's her domain. So what's wrong with adding flowers, frills, pastels and lots of pink? In fact, many men are proud when someone notes that their home has that "feminine touch." It shows they've found someone who cares.

Courtesy of Wellborn Cabinet, Inc.

A lot of love was put into the details of this kitchen, from the abstract floral stained glass windows to the tri-colored tile work on counter and backsplash and cutout detailing in the island woodwork. A neutral sage green paint for the walls and natural maple cabinetry provide a warm setting for the fancy work.

Courtesy of Wellborn Cabinet, Inc.

Pickle finish on maple adds a blonde complement to rose-colored walls in this delicate kitchen. A leaded glass panel in the corner wall cabinet completes the feminine look.

Courtesy of Congoleum Corp.

This designer went for understated, painting beaded cabinetry and wood trim beige, underscoring them with "Cheyenne" resilient sheet flooring.

Contrast is key to this kitchen's charm—dark green and gold wallpaper, window treatments, and countertop against stark white cabinetry. The "Keynote" resilient sheet flooring plays off both themes, and rounds up scattered red accents.

Courtesy of Congoleum Corp.

"Floral Lace" resilient sheet flooring and soft wallpaper and window treatments add a feminine touch to this spacious kitchen.

Courtesy of Congoleum Corp.

Soft blue lines in floor and curtain provide a color foundation for the gentle mural behind the range top. This is a very understated kitchen, with muted frost finish on the cabinets against white stucco walls and white appliances.

Courtesy of Fieldstone Cabinetry, Inc.

A upgrade in range hood can make all the difference in a kitchen, here serving as a central focus point. "Mountain Oak" resilient wood plank flooring sets off the light tones of peach cabinetry and sage accents.

Neutral tones allow accent objects to draw attention.

Archways above and below provide a hearth theme in this cool blue kitchen. From the do-it-yourself resilient sheet flooring, through the chrome accents, to the snowflake border paper, the color theme creates a clean, modern environment for preparing food and enjoying it.

Courtesy of Lori Engelhart

Clean, off-white cabinets allow star appliances, a floral wallpaper, and a fancy corner unit to predominate. A television on a rotating stand accommodates shifting audiences, be it the cook or those assembled at a nearby seating area. A second sink allows people to fix drinks or help out without getting in the way.

Soft blue lines in floor and curtain provide a color foundation for the gentle mural behind the range top. This is a very understated kitchen, with muted frost finish on the cabinets against white stucco walls and white appliances.

This is a homey kitchen space, with decorative wallpaper and warm natural tones to make it cozy.

Soothing peach tones with floral accents give a decidedly feminine touch to this kitchen by Jean M. Buchen, CKD. A big island, complete with wet sink, wine rack, and a stove for the teapot insure that nobody stays thirsty long here.

White makes it bright in this neat assembly of cabinets, including a handy wine rack on the island. The flooring is laminate "Golden Beech."

FUSION OF IDEAS

Here, finally, is a mixed bag of great kitchens; rooms that drew their inspiration from old and new, exotic and down-home. They defy definition, while creating their own character. Some take a decidedly Southwestern bent, while others head to the Far East. There's a little sprinkling of Shaker and Mission styles, along with Mod. These are all marvelous kitchens that deny categories. So let each one speak for itself, and enjoy.

Courtesy of Aristokraft®

A few touches like wicker window shades and floor mat and a geometric range hood create an Asian atmosphere. Natural wood trim and insert crown with rope molding add subtle elegance.

Courtesy of Wood-Mode Inc.

Here's a great place to be—an adobe kitchen that leads straight to the walled patio. Southwestern flair is added with carved molding on the upper cabinets, terra-cotta tiles, bits of lace, big clay bowls, and touches of wrought iron.

Old wood structural elements contrast with modern appliances and lighting fixtures. A happy medium was struck with the cabinetry—an antique gray finish on bead board doors below, off white cabinets above. Real metal and porcelain stone tiles by Crossville are used on the checkerboard splashback that wraps the countertops

Courtesy of Wood-Mode Inc.

Details meant everything to this kitchen designer, from the stained-glass window to the wrought iron over the stove. A spice finish on the cabinetry adds warmth, as do terra-cotta tiles.

Courtesy of Wood-Mode Inc.

Courtesy of Aristokraft®

A log cabin gets a refined kitchen, with laminate cabinets and oversize-tiles on the stove backsplash and countertops. A high back on the island work station doubles as seat back for a cozy booth seating area.

Updating a charming 1918 cottage, designer Gerard Ciccarello used Heritage maple cabinetry with an ivory finish and moss green accents. For interest, the island was constructed in cherry with a white glaze. A special corner plate rack was designed for the owner's plate collection.

Courtesy of Covenant Kitchens & Baths, Inc.

Courtesy of Cross Interiors

Created for a brand-new home, interest here was inserted with a bay window at the main sink and a large bay seating area in the breakfast room. The cook top was a focal point, designed with a brick facade and hand-painted tiles. Brick was repeated on the fireplace and inset under the table to withstand wear and tear. The oak flooring was designed on the diagonal to visually widen the long room. To differentiate, rift oak was selected for the cabinetry. A volume of fabric on the windows and numerous pillows on the cushioned window seat soften the acoustics of the kitchen immensely.

Here's a cook who put first priority on the oven and range, with a big hood to top it all off. Natural finish cabinetry frames the workplace and an oversize checkerboard floor underlines it all.

A beamed, wood ceiling and stucco walls gave this kitchen designer an ideal place to play. This kitchen wends its way from a handsome stove work area to a corner nook with window to a fantastic dining hutch/buffet unit, all in matching-finish cabinetry. A natural stone floor completes the luxury.

Lighting in glass-fronted cabinets and under the upper cabinets make up for small windows in this well-appointed kitchen. A unique tile pattern in the backsplash is mirrored in tiles on the range hood. Another nice touch is the beveled wood edge surrounding the countertops and island work station.

An interesting, two-tone countertop ties a china hutch and appliances together. Another interesting feature is the range hood, which mimics the wall cabinets and provides a display shelf.

Courtesy of Wood-Mode Inc.

A natural finish allows the bold grains of hickory to shine against a rich backdrop of wallpaper and a central tile mosaic above the sink.

Courtesy of Wellborn Cabinet, Inc.

Regina Bilotta and Eric Witkin wanted to seamlessly blend a new extension into the pre-existing Arts and Crafts period architecture and furnishings in their home. A team of twelve Bilotta kitchen designers collaborated, choosing simple cherry cabinetry with shaker-style cabinet doors customized with rails by Rutt. Granite countertops were paired with a marble backsplash. The limestone floor is sprinkled with the color rust, which is picked up in the cabinets, bringing it all together.

Courtesy of Bilotta Home Center, Inc.

Courtesy of Summitville Tiles, Inc.

Delft blue accents on decorative tiles adorn this kitchen, with decorative murals on the backsplash and a rope twist along the edges. Neutral cabinetry and tile flooring complete this first-class look.

Courtesy of Wood-Mode Inc.

Carved grape molding surrounds two island work areas as well as an impressive stucco range hood. The natural wood and clay colors are complemented by a gray countertop and splashes of red and green paint.

Courtesy of Kountry Kraft

Beautiful integrity of design was incorporated here by designer Jean M. Buchen, CKD, from the wood-tone details on the cabinets, range hood, and under the counter, to the green ceramic pieces scattered throughout the kitchen. A moveable, butcher-block counter and oval rag rug create an old-time atmosphere.

Photography by Keith Lanpher/Courtesy of Fisher Group

A New Orleans feeling was created by using two-toned cabinets in the Louis Phillipe style. The dark green granite countertop ties in to the mural of Tunisian musicians in a subtropical setting and the irregular black glass accents in the backsplash. The telephone desk with working drawer is a piece of engineering magic on the part of the cabinet-maker.

Laser technology was used to create this hardwood floor with inlaid medallion. Old fashioned technology created the little angel poised on the countertop.

Courtesy of Legendary Hardwood Floors

Black trim and wood tones tie this kitchen and an outer office area together. Playing a neutral partner is "Marblesque" resilient sheet flooring.

Courtesy of Congoleum Corp.

Courtesy of Congoleum Corp.

White cabinetry is complemented by matching appliances, while a dark countertop ties them all together. A wrought iron shelving unit dominates one wall and "Concorde Quarry" resilient sheet flooring provides the solid look of stone underfoot.

Cream-colored flat-faced cabinets create a dream-like atmosphere in this room, highlighted by the angled ceiling and an angular accent line in the tile backsplash. The colors in the granite countertop are repeated in the backsplash accent, the surrounding laminate countertop, and the wall paint color.

Photography by Keith Lanpher/Courtesy of Fisher Group

Black, white, and just a bit of brown to tone it down. This kitchen could take on any accent color—be it red, blue, or banana yellow—in dining sets, dish towels, and the like.

Courtesy of Congoleum Corp.

Courtesy of Congoleum Corp.

Simple cabinetry and fancy window-panes offer timeless good taste. The blue-green countertop is carried through with a picture frame and accents in the resilient sheet flooring.

Facing cabinetry flush with the wall lends itself to interesting effects, like this sunken desk area in the kitchen. Cabinet, wall, and countertop colors are coordinated for beautiful effect.

Courtesy of Plain & Fancy

An arched range hood and echoing tile backsplash take center stage in this kitchen, framed by sage green cabinets. Understated Oregano glaze fills out the rest of the kitchen.

Courtesy of Fieldstone Cabinetry, Inc.

Stucco walls and range hood blend beautifully with a spicy wood-tone finish on the cabinetry. Blue countertops add a nice splash of color.

Courtesy of Wood-Mode Inc.

Borrowing design principals of balance and simplicity from the East, this uncomplicated kitchen has subtle features that optimize storage and work space. Bird's-eye maple panels and frosted glass squares set into bisque-stained maple cabinetry provide symmetry to the design, punctuated by a clean, black counter and matching granite sink. Custom refrigerator panels seamlessly blend the appliance in with the rest of the room.

Courtesy of Plain & Fancy

A creative faux-painted inlay wood floor of maple makes its mark on this kitchen, topped by a table/island with granite counter and wet sink. Classic white cabinetry and a professional, stainless steel oven and range unit dominate the walls.

Courtesy of Blue Bell Kitchens

Oak cabinetry creates a warm country atmosphere, dressed up with leaded glass inserts, customized tile backsplash and countertop, and a stained glass lighting unit. The cabinets, in classic frame-and-panel style, were finished in the warm honey tone of Cider.

Courtesy of Merillat Industries

A light, country feeling is created with painted cabinetry and southern pine beaded ceiling panels. A fanciful light fixture and a filmy window swag complete the scene.

Courtesy of Southern Pine Council

Courtesy of Star Mark, Inc.

White makes it bright, helping this small kitchen become a little showplace. Mission-inspired glass insert doors open things up further. Eyebrow valances frame open spaces and attractive stack molding tops off the look.

Courtesy of Star Mark, Inc.

The nutmeg color is carried through on the range hood to complete the classic lines of this cherry cabinetry. A drop ceiling over the island and decorative ceiling fixtures add a nice touch.

Courtesy of Fieldstone Cabinetry, Inc.

The vibrant personality of hickory highlights this hard-working kitchen design.

Courtesy of IXL Cabinets

Modern accents like the range hood, an angular teapot, and contemporary artwork contrast with traditional plantation hardwood cabinetry and a polished wood floor.

Resource Guide

American Woodmark
3102 Shawnee Drive
Winchester, VA 22601
540-665-9100
www.woodmark.com

Aristokraft®
One Master Brand Cabinets Dr.
Jasper, IN 47546
812-482-2527
aoksales@psci.net
www.aristokraft.com

Aristokraft is a leading manufacturer of quality kitchen, bath, and home cabinetry. From the traditional beauty of oak to the radiant elegance of cherry, the company offers more than forty different styles and a multitude of accessories.

Bilotta Home Center, Inc.
564 Mamaroneck Avenue
Mamaroneck, NY 10543
914-381-7734/Fax: 381-0668

With showrooms in Mamaroneck, Briarcliff, and Bedford, this company has been designing and installing dream kitchens for over forty years. Bilotta is Westchester's exclusive Rutt Cabinetry designer and installer and also features Siematic and Wood-Mode brand custom cabinetry.

Blue Bell Kitchens
1104 Bethlehem Pike
P.O. Box 371
Springhouse, PA 19477
215-646-5442/Fax: 646-3330
peter@bluebellkitchens.com
www.bluebellkitchens.com

This group of talented and dedicated designers specializes in period-inspired cabinetry and interior design. They serve the Mid-Atlantic region, creating detailed, functional kitchens that compliment the architectural or period style of the home.

Brookhaven Cabinetry
One Second Street
Kreamer, PA 17833
570-374-2711/Fax: 372-1422
www.wood-mode.com

A companion line of Wood-Mode, Brookhaven provides semi-custom cabinetry with frame and frameless construction choices in styles ranging from country to contemporary and traditional to high-tech, with finishes that provide an ideal blend of toughness and beauty.

Jean M. Buchen, CKD
P.O. Box 570
Newmanstown, PA 17073
610-589-4575
www.kountrykraft.com

A certified kitchen designer, Jean M. Buchen is an in-house designer for Kountry Kraft cabinetry company.

bulthaup corporation
The Prince Bldg., Suite 306
578 Broadway
New York, NY 10012
212-966-7183/Fax: 966-0790
bulthaupUS@aol.com

This German based company concentrates on function of design for aesthetically pleasing, ergonomically correct kitchens, with an accent on minimalism.

Congoleum Corp.
P.O. Box 8116
Trenton, NJ 08650-0116
800-274-3266
www.congoleum.com

Congoleum Corporation is one of the nation's leading manufacturers of resilient sheet and tile, resilient wood plank, and laminate flooring. Based in Mercerville, New Jersey, Congoleum's origins extend back more than one hundred years. Congoleum resilient flooring products are designed and manufactured in the United States, with manufacturing facilities in Trenton, New Jersey; Marcus Hook, Pennsylvania, and Cedarhurst, Maryland.

Covenant Kitchens & Baths, Inc.
1871 Boston Post Road
Westbrook, CT 06498
860-399-6241
covenantkitchens@snet.com

Designers Joseph B. Ciccarello and Gerard Ciccarello are both kitchen designers certified by the National Kitchen and Bath Association.

Cross Interiors
6712 Colbath Avenue
Van Nuys, CA 91405
818-988-2047/Fax: 785-8383
cherylcaseyross@crossinteriors.com
www.crossinteriors.com

Cheryl Casey Ross is a Certified Interior Designer and a member of ASID, IIDA, and an AIA/SFV Professional Affiliate. She has clients all over the United States, has won numerous design awards, and has been published in over eighty magazines and newspapers.

Crossville Porcelain Stone/USA
P.O. Box 1168
Crossville, TN 38557
931-484-2110/Fax: 484-8418
www.crossville-ceramics.com

Founded in 1986, Crossville Porcelain Stone/ USA is the largest domestic manufacturer of large-size porcelain stone tile for both residential and contract applications. High-fired, through-color porcelain tile is more durable than natural stone and virtually immune to scratches, stains, and fading.

Distinctive Kitchen & Bath Interiors
5891 Firestone Drive
Syracuse, NY 13206
315-434-9011/Fax: 434-9013
www.distinctiveinteriors.com

Design consultant Brian K. Fagan has been creating kitchen and bath designs for central New York clients since 1990. His designs have been featured in *Better Homes & Gardens* and in *Kitchens by Professional Designers*.

Dutch Made Custom Cabinetry Inc.
P.O. Box 310
Graybill, IN 46741
219-657-3311/ Fax: 657-5778
dutchmade@ctinet.com
www.dutchmade.com

Lori Engelhart, CKD
Stock Lumber
1735 Kramer Street
La Crosse, WI 54603
800-658-9025/608-781-3900 ext. 213
LoriCkd@aol.com

Lori Engelhart is a Certified Kitchen Designer for Stock Lumber's "Cabinet Gallery." She works closely with clients, and uses a computer graphics program to show homeowners views of their kitchen from different perspectives, allowing them to visualize her design concepts.

Euro Kitchen & Bath Corp.
465 Forest Avenue
Laguna Beach, CA 92651
877-436-2842/Fax: 497-4577
sales@eurokitchens.com
www.eurokitchens.com

Claude and Fari Moritz are both Belgian licensed architects who specialize in custom kitchen design. Their California business is over twenty years old.

Fieldstone Cabinetry, Inc.
600 E. 48th St. N.
Sioux Falls, SD 57104
inquire@FieldstoneCabinetry.com
www.FieldstoneCabinetry.com

Fieldstone personalizes your cabinetry for your lifestyle, with an extensive menu of accessory, design, and fashion element options.

Fisher Group
4119 Chatelain Road
Annandale, VA 22003
703-750-1151/Fax: 256-2516
www.design-build-renovate.com

Designer Peggy Fisher, CR, CKD, is an Allied Member of ASID. She has twenty years of award-winning experience in new and renovation projects, and offers architectural and interior design services for large additions and kitchen and bath design.

Forest Floors Inc.
295 Centre Avenue
Rockland, MA 02370
877-328-1778/Fax: 878-1446
www.forest-floors.com

Forest Floors, Inc. offers wood flooring from around the world in a tremendous selection of colors, textures, and designs. High quality installations are available in a local area as well as borders, inlays, and personalized floor inserts.

Four Seasons Sunrooms
5005 Veterans Memorial Highway
Holbrook, New York 11741
1-800-368-7732
info@four-seasons-sunrooms.com
www.four-seasons-sunrooms.com

Four Seasons Sunrooms designs, builds, and ships its exclusive product line to more than three hundred independently owned and operated franchises and dealers in over thirty countries. Their sunrooms and skylights are designed to control both solar heat gain and winter heat loss in such extreme climates as Canada and Alaska, Arizona and the Middle East.

Hanford Cabinet & Woodworking
102 Ingham Hill Road
Old Saybrook, CT 06475
860-388-5055/Fax: 388-6204
hanfordcabinet@snet.net
www.hanfordcabinet.com

In business for two decades, Hanford is a custom design and fabrication firm specializing in high-end cabinetry for the home and office.

The Hardwood Council
P.O. Box 525
Oakmont, PA 15139
412-281-4980/Fax: 323-9334
www.hardwoodcouncil.com

The Hardwood Council produces free technical literature on working with North American hardwoods. Interior designers, architects, builders, and remodelers are invited to view and order the council's literature on their website.

Barbara Herr, CKD
141 W. Market Street
Marietta, PA 17547
717-426-2287/Fax: 426-3005

Barbara Herr, CKD, has been designing professionally for over twenty years. She fulfills her clients' needs, wants, and desires by blending art, architecture, practical efficiency, and their own style into a functional kitchen that just feels right to be in.

Dee Hurst-Funk, CKD
P.O. Box 570
Newmanstown, PA 17073
610-589-4575
www.kountrykraft.com

A certified kitchen designer, Dee Hurst-Funk is an in-house designer for Kountry Kraft cabinetry company.

IXL Cabinets
16803 Dallas Parkway
Addison, TX 75001
214-887-2000/Fax: 887-2434
cabmail@armstrong.com
www.ixlcabinets.com

Triangle Pacific Corp. (an Armstrong company) is a leading manufacturer of kitchen cabinets in the United States. Its IXL Cabinets Division produces more than two million cabinets annually, offering a variety of door styles, species, and finishes.

Jim Bishop Cabinets, Inc.
P.O. Box 11424
Montgomery, AL 36111
334-288-1381/Fax: 281-3950
www.jimbishopcabinets.com

Jim Bishop founded the company in 1964. Door styles are available in oak, maple, poplar, hickory, thermofoil and melamine, with six standard finishes available as well as glazes, semi-opaque base coats, crackle, edge wear, and veiling.

John's Custom Floors, Inc.
231 Nevada Street
Redwood City, CA 94062
650-367-9217/Fax: 367-8052
www.johnscustomfloors.com

John Paulazzo is a member of the National Wood Flooring Association and is known for his quality custom installations throughout the San Francisco Bay Area. He has over twenty-five years of experience in the wood flooring industry.

Kitchen Blueprints
4231-D Princess Place Drive
Wilmington, NC 28405
910-763-2536
info@KitchenBlueprints.com

Company president and owner Cynthia Sporre, CKD, has more than nineteen years of experience in kitchen design. She has particular expertise in high-end lines, and focuses designs on style, historical period, or international looks, working with forty cabinet lines.

Kitchens Unique, Inc.
118 Depot Drive
Madison, MS 39110
601-898-1199/Fax: 898-1190
melkitch@kitchensunique.com
www.kitchensunique.com

Mellany C. Kitchens, CKD, has been in business since 1990, when she began her own cabinet manufacturing facility. She specializes in kitchen design with emphasis on the high-end clientele, and is past-president of her local NKBA chapter.

Kountry Kraft
P.O. Box 570
291 South Sheridan Road
Newmanstown, PA 17073
610-589-4575
www.kountrykraft.com

Manufacturing custom-made cabinetry since 1959. Kountry Kraft's desire has been to provide a high-quality custom product, to deliver it on schedule, and to price it fairly.

Laufen International Ceramic Tile
P.O. Box 570
Tulsa, OK 74101-0570
800-758-8453
usa.laufen.com

Laufen Ceramic Tile is a leading domestic manufacturer of design-oriented tile.

Legendary Hardwood Floors
601 S. 21st Street
Terre Haute, IN 47803
812-232-3372/Fax: 234-6794

Founder Chuck Crispin learned hardwood floor restoration from a master, and was one of the first people in the United States to apply laser technology to inlaid wood flooring.

Merillat Industries
P.O. Box 1946
Adrian, MI 49221
800-575-8763, ext. 6557
www.merillat.com

Merillat has been providing quality cabinetry and storage solutions for the nation's homes for over fifty years.

Plain & Fancy Custom Cabinetry
Route 501 & Oak Street
P.O. Box 519
Schaefferstown, PA 17088
800-447-9006
www.plainfancycabinetry.com

Plain & Fancy, a family-run company for thirty-one years, stands for quality workmanship at a surprisingly affordable price. Each cabinet is built using time-tested methods: mortise and tenon construction and dovetail drawers.

Poulin Design Remodeling
2426 Washington NE
Albuquerque, NM 87710
505-883-4040
www.remodelingmadeeasy.com

Tom Poulin, CGR, in business for seventeen years, was named Remodeler of the Year in 1998 by the Remodelers™ Council. He utilizes the latest products and technology, including computer imaging to enable clients to see their homes redesigned before carpenters actually show up at their door.

Restore 'N More, Inc.
25 S. Main Street
Manheim, PA 17545
717-664-7575/Fax: 664-7577
dbaer@restorenmore.com

This full-service restoration firm specializes in historic restoration, custom additions, and custom renovations. In business since 1987, the firm is best known for restoration expertise in Pennsylvania-German and English structures built prior to the mid-19th century, as well as its sensitivity to incorporating modern amenities into the historic home.

Rutt of Atlanta
351 Peachtree Hills Ave, N.E.
Suite 413
Atlanta, GA 30305
404-264-9698/Fax: 264-0346

With more than eighty-eight years of combined design experience, a talented team of Certified Kitchen Designers can work from scratch to create an entire space or support other professionals in achieving their vision. Rutt of Atlanta combines the long-term quality and integrity of a national brand with the flexibility of your favorite local woodworker for custom cabinetry that is guaranteed for life.

Schenck and Company Fine Wood Floors
910 Winston Street
P.O. Box 70007
Houston, TX 77270
713-266-7608/Fax: 863-1547

Schenck and Company has been creating fine inlaid, patterned, and rustic plank flooring in some of the finest homes in the Houston area since 1982.

Southern Forest Products Association
P.O. Box 641700
Kenner, LA 70064-1700
504-443-4464
www.southernpine.com

Southern Pine Council is a joint promotional program supported by producing members of the Southern Forest Products Association and the Southeastern Lumber Manufacturers Association. Both associations represent southern pine lumber manufacturers.

Star Mark, Inc.
600 E. 48th St. N.
Sioux Falls, SD 57104
605-335-8600
inquire@StarMarkCabinetry.com
www.StarMarkCabinetry.com

Fine StarMark cabinetry offers choices to let you express yourself with full creative freedom. Choose from a comprehensive selection of woods, finishes, accessories, fashion elements, and true custom options.

Summitville Tiles, Inc.
P.O. Box 73
Summitville, OH 43962
330-223-1511/Fax: 223-1414
info@sumitville.com
www.summitville.com

Manufacturing tile since 1912, Summitville Tiles produces a wide variety of floor, wall, and decorative tiles/murals and a complete line of grouts, mortars, epoxies, furan, latex, waterproofing materials, and tile care products.

Victoria Benatar Urban
220 E 65th St. #15-B
New York, NY 10021
212-755-0525
vbu@e-arquitectura.com
www.e-arquitectura.com

Architect Victoria Benatar Urban develops architecture, interior design, digital and urban design projects in New York, Miami, and Caracas, Venezuela. She was an adjunct professor at the Columbia University Graduate School of Architecture, Planning, and Preservation, and works as a part-time faculty member at Parsons School of Design. She has a Master of Science degree in architecture and urban design from Columbia University.

Viking Range Corporation
1-888-845-4641
www.vikingrange.com

Viking outfits the professional kitchen with cooking, ventilation, cleanup, and refrigeration products, as well as outdoor grills.

Weather Shield Windows & Doors
P.O. Box 309
Medford, WI 54451
800-477-6808
www.weathershield.com

One of the nation's largest window manufacturers, Weather Shield Windows & Doors is based in Medford, Wisconsin, and operates plants in Medford, Ladysmith, and Greenwood, Wisconsin and in Logan, Utah.

Wellborn Cabinet, Inc.
38669 Highway 77
Ashland, AL 36251
256-354-7022
www.wellborncabinet.com

Wellborn Cabinet offers over a hundred different door styles, all hand-sanded, and hand finished in a choice of over fifty finishes. More than seven hundred accessory cabinets are available for the kitchen or for any room of the home.

Wood-Mode Inc.
One Second Street
Kreamer, PA 17833
570-374-2711/Fax: 372-1422
www.wood-mode.com

The company features a full line of custom, built-in cabinetry for every room of the home. Backed by a lifetime limited warranty, the line features two basic construction options—framed and frameless—in more than ninety door styles and one hundred finishes, as well as a wide selection of options to maximize storage.

YesterTec
P.O. Box 190
Center Valley, PA 18034
610-838-1194/Fax: 838-1937

Yorktowne Cabinets
P.O. Box 231
Red Lion, PA 17356
717-244-4011/Fax: 244-5497
cabinets@yorktwn.com
www.yorktowneinc.com

A member of the Elkay Cabinet Group, Yorktowne is celebrating its ninety-second year as one of the nation's largest producers of stock and semi-custom cabinets. Their product line features tiered pricing that gives consumers multiple choices across a beautiful spectrum of door styles, finishes, features, and options.